T0413419

PHYSICAL SCIENCE

The Mystery of Magnets

PAMELA BLISS

PICTURE CREDITS
Cover: © David Parker/IMI/Univ. of Birmingham High, TC Consortium/Science Photo Library. Page 1 © Tek Image/Photo Researchers, Inc.; pages 2–3 © Chase Swift/Corbis; pages 4–5 © Jack Finch/Photo Researchers, Inc.; page 5 © Mug Shots/Corbis; pages 6, 26 Robb Gregg/Robb Gregg Studios; page 7 © John Clarke/Peter Arnold; pages 8, 27 (lower), 28, 29 Sharon Hoogstraten; pages 9, 10 (lower), 12 (top), 24–25 Precision Graphics; page 10 (top) © Tom Pantages/Tom Pantages; page 11 © Spencer Grant/Photo Researchers, Inc.; page 12 (lower), 22 (lower left), 22 (lower center), 22 (lower right) © Hemera; page 13 © Christoph Burki/Getty Images; page 14 © Miles Ertman/Masterfile; page 15 © Sinclair Stammers/Science Photo Library; page 16 © Stan Sherer/Stan Sherer; page 17 © David Young-Wolff/PhotoEdit; page 18 © Tony Freeman/PhotoEdit; page 19 © Lawrence Manning/Corbis; page 20 © James Leynse/Corbis SABA; page 21 © NASA; page 23 © Simon Fraser/Science Photo Library; page 27 (top) © Bettmann/Corbis; page 31 © Bill Aron/PhotoEdit.

Neither the publisher nor the author shall be liable for any damage that may be caused or sustained or result from conducting any of the activities in this book without specifically following instructions, undertaking the activities without proper supervision, or failing to comply with the cautions contained in the book.

Produced through the worldwide resources of the National Geographic Society, John M. Fahey, Jr., President and Chief Executive Officer; Gilbert M. Grosvenor, Chairman of the Board; Nina D. Hoffman, Executive Vice President and President, Books and Education Publishing Group.

PROGRAM DEVELOPER
Kate Boehm Jerome

ART DIRECTION
Daniel Banks, Project Design Company

CONSULTANT/REVIEWER
Dr. James Shymansky, E. Desmond Lee Professor of Science Education, University of Missouri-St. Louis

BOOK DEVELOPMENT
Navta Associates

Published by the National Geographic Society
1145 17th Street, N.W.
Washington, D.C. 20036-4688

ISBN: 978-0-7922-4581-0
ISBN: 0-7922-4581-4
5 6 7 8 9 10 11 12 13 19 18 17 16 15 14 13
Printed in the United States of America

Title page photo: Electric current in the large disc (superconductor) produces a magnetic field that repels the small magnet and makes it float. This technology is what makes a maglev train float above the track.

PREPARED BY NATIONAL GEOGRAPHIC SCHOOL PUBLISHING
Ericka Markman, Senior Vice President and President, Children's Books and Education Publishing Group; Steve Mico, Vice President, Editorial Director; Rosemary Baker, Executive Editor; Barbara Seeber, Editorial Manager; Jim Hiscott, Design Manager; Kristin Hanneman, Illustrations Manager; Matt Wascavage, Manager of Publishing Services; Sean Philpotts, Production Manager.

MANUFACTURING AND QUALITY MANAGEMENT
Christopher A. Liedel, Chief Financial Officer; Phillip L. Schlosser, Director; Clifton M. Brown, Manager.

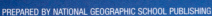

Scientists believe that Earth's magnetic field helps guide the migrations of birds.

Contents

A Magnetic Light Show

The northern lights glow near Fairbanks, Alaska.

What are these colors glowing in the northern sky? This amazing light show is called the aurora borealis, or the northern lights.

In the far northern part of Earth, you might see the northern lights. It has to be a dark, clear night. You have to be far away from city lights. Then, if the time is right, the sky may glow with the greens and reds of the northern lights.

You may not be in the right place to see the northern lights. But you have seen the force that causes them—**magnetism**—in action. Magnetism is a force that pushes or pulls on things.

This is a book about **magnets** and magnetism. A magnet is an object that has the power to pull things toward it. Did you think that magnets were just holding notes on your refrigerator door? Not so. Read on to see how magnets and magnetism work all around us.

Chapter 1

Magnets and Magnetism

The Invisible Force

If you tried balancing like this with your friends, what would happen? You'd fall, of course! Why don't these tiny acrobats fall? They have a special invisible quality—called magnetism.

What is special about magnets? Magnets have the power to **attract**, or pull, things made of iron and certain other metals.

The pull of a magnet is an invisible force. You cannot see any strings or wires. You can only observe movement. You see the magnet pull an object toward it. If you hold the magnet or the object, you can also feel the pull. An object that is pulled by a magnet is **magnetic**.

What Is Magnetic?

What kinds of things are magnetic? As you know, iron objects are magnetic. So are objects made of steel. That's because steel is made from iron.

What objects in your home are made of iron or steel? You can probably guess some of them: paper clips, the refrigerator door, knives, tools. All of these objects can be pulled by a magnet.

The magnet's force works through the paper. It attracts the paper clips underneath.

What a Magnet Can Do

A very strong magnet can pull an object from far away. When a magnet is weaker, the object must be closer to be pulled by the magnet's force.

What if something lies between the magnet and a magnetic object? Can the force of the magnet be felt then? The answer depends on two things: the strength of the magnet and the material that lies between.

For example, the force of a refrigerator magnet can work through a piece of paper. That's why it's used to hold up paper notes. But the force may not work through several sheets of paper. That requires a stronger magnet.

Pull and Push

A magnet will attract a magnetic object. But what happens if you place two magnets together? You might feel the magnets attract each other. Or you might feel them **repel**, or push away, each other.

When will magnets attract each other? When will they repel each other? The answers depend on the positions of the magnets' **poles**. A pole is an area of a magnet where its magnetism is strongest. Each magnet has two different poles.

From Pole to Pole

Every magnet has a **north pole** and a **south pole**. Like poles repel each other. Unlike poles attract each other.

If you hold the *north* pole of one magnet near the *north* pole of another magnet, then the like poles will be next to each other. You will feel the magnets repel, or push away from each other.

If you hold the *north* pole of one magnet near the *south* pole of another magnet, then the unlike poles will be next to each other. You will feel the magnets attract, or pull toward each other.

Thinking Like a Scientist: Inferring

Magnetism is an invisible force. The only way to prove an object is magnetic is to hold a magnet near it. But if you don't have a magnet, you can **infer** whether or not an object is magnetic. When you infer, you make a decision based on past experience. You have already observed many magnets in your everyday life. Based on what you've seen, can you infer which of these objects are magnetic?

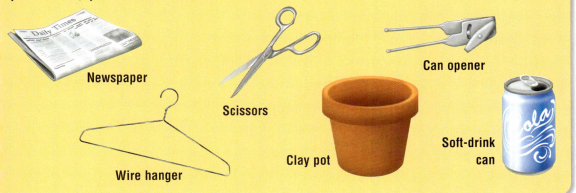

Newspaper

Scissors

Can opener

Wire hanger

Clay pot

Soft-drink can

Magnet Shapes

Where are the poles on a magnet? It depends on the shape of the magnet. Three common magnet shapes are the horseshoe, bar, and ring.

The poles on a horseshoe magnet are at its ends. The magnetism is strongest there. The same is true of a bar magnet. But a ring magnet has no ends. Its poles are on its two flat sides.

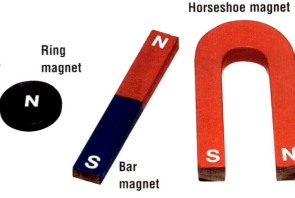

Horseshoe magnet

Ring magnet

Bar magnet

Magnetic Fields

A magnet has an invisible region of force around it. This region is called its **magnetic field**. That's how a magnet attracts objects that are not touching it. A magnetic object just has to come within a magnet's magnetic field.

The picture below shows the magnetic field of a bar magnet.

The lines are drawn flat on the page. But a magnetic field is not flat. It wraps all around a magnet on every side.

Differently shaped magnets have differently shaped magnetic fields. Look at the horseshoe magnet at the right. Bits of iron are lining up in its magnetic field. They help you see where the magnetic field lies. Most iron bits clump where magnetism is strongest— at the poles.

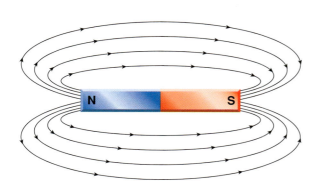

The lines show the magnetic field of the bar magnet. Look at where the lines are closest together. That's where the magnetic force is strongest. The arrows show the direction of the force.

Can you see where the magnetic field is strongest on a horseshoe magnet?

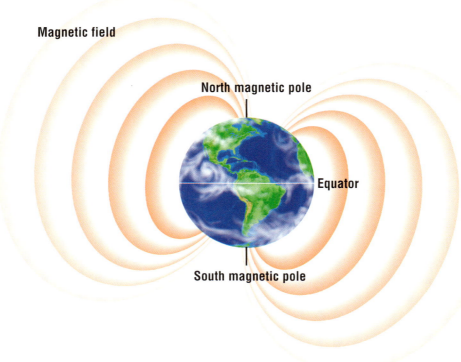

Magnetic field

North magnetic pole

Equator

South magnetic pole

The magnetic field around Earth is strongest at the north and south magnetic poles.

A Huge Magnet: Earth

Did you know that Earth itself is a magnet? At the center of Earth is a core of hot iron and nickel. These two materials are both magnetic.

Like any magnet, Earth has a north pole and a south pole. (However, these are different from the geographic places we call the North and South Pole.) Earth's magnetism is strongest at the north magnetic and south magnetic poles.

A **compass** is a tool that uses Earth's magnetism. The needle in a compass is magnetic. So it is pulled along the lines of Earth's magnetic field. The needle of the compass lines up north-south. So whether you're a sailor or a hiker, you can use a compass to chart your course.

The Magnetic Light Show

Think back to the northern lights shown on page 4. They happen because of Earth's magnetic field. The sun sends millions of tiny particles out into space. Some particles become trapped in Earth's magnetic field. They are pulled toward the north magnetic or south magnetic pole. As they move, they bump and ram into particles in Earth's air. They collide so hard that they give off light energy. We can see this light energy. The light energy becomes the colors of the northern lights.

Stay **Tuned!**

Magnetic Mysteries

Humans are not the only ones to use Earth's magnetism to find direction. Animals may use it, too. For example, some birds **migrate**. This means they fly back and forth from one area to another every year. Scientists think birds may sense Earth's north-south magnetic field. They may use it to help find their way.

Honeybees also use magnetism to find direction. A honeybee will do a "dance." Its movements show other honeybees the direction in which they can find food. This dance is affected by Earth's magnetic field. Scientists continue to study how honeybees and birds use Earth's magnetic field.

Honeybee

Chapter 2

Exploring Magnetism

Unlocking the Mystery

The mystery of magnets fascinated the people living in an area of ancient Greece called Magnesia. Why did some metals stick to certain rocks? Was it magic?

This area, once known as Magnesia, is located in the mountains of central Greece.

People noticed magnetism thousands of years ago. They wondered why some rocks could pull other rocks. What mysterious force was at work?

The Greeks Name It

Long ago in Greece, people became interested in magnetism. The word "magnet" comes from a place in ancient Greece. There was an area in Greece called Magnesia. A metal we now call magnetite was found there. Magnetite is a magnet.

One legend tells about a shepherd in Magnesia who felt his iron staff stick to the ground. It had been pulled by magnetite rocks. This shepherd's name was Magnes.

The Greeks learned that rocks containing magnetite attracted things that contained iron. Many people thought it must be magic. Some of them began to collect and trade pieces of magnetite.

Magnetite

The Chinese Compass

The people in ancient China discovered magnetism before the Greeks did. The Chinese noticed that magnetic rocks were pulled in a north-south direction.

The Chinese were probably the first people to use compasses. There is a Chinese legend about the compass. It tells about the Chinese emperor Hwang-ti, who lived more than 4,000 years ago. During a battle, a thick fog surrounded the emperor and his army. Hwang-ti found his way through the fog by using a kind of compass. It was a piece of magnetite in the arm of a small statue. The magnetite caused the arm to point in a north-south direction.

Later the Chinese made an actual compass by placing a spoon made of magnetite on a plate. The spoon could turn around on its rounded bottom. It would turn until it lay in a north-south direction.

In time the Chinese learned to make iron needles magnetic by rubbing magnetite against them. They invented another kind of compass with a magnetic iron needle. The needle floated and turned on water.

Much later, Europeans learned about compasses from the Chinese. European explorers, such as Christopher Columbus, used compasses to guide their ships.

Chinese spoon compass

A modern compass works like those made long ago.

The compasses helped them sail to faraway lands such as America.

Gilbert's Discovery

Many people still thought magnets had magical powers. They believed magnets could cure some diseases. They even thought magnets could help couples have happy marriages!

Then about 400 years ago, a scientist named William Gilbert studied magnets. Gilbert experimented with magnetite and compass needles. He observed an important fact: The magnetite attracted the needles much like Earth attracted a compass needle. Gilbert wondered what caused this. From his observations, Gilbert concluded that Earth itself must be a giant magnet. He was right!

Word Power

In England, people began to call magnetite "lodestone." The word "lode" meant "to lead." Lodestone could help lead people by showing them which direction was north.

Oersted's Discovery

Some great discoveries in science are made because of luck. A scientist is in the right place at the right time to see something happen. This is what happened when the connection between magnetism and electricity was discovered.

The discovery happened almost 200 years ago. Hans Christian Oersted was a scientist in Denmark in 1820. He was teaching a class about electricity. He moved an electric wire near a compass. The needle of the compass moved! It was attracted by the wire.

Oersted was lucky to have noticed the compass reacting to the wire. But he was also smart. He soon figured out an important rule: Electricity running through a wire creates a magnetic field around the wire. This connection between electricity and magnetism is known as **electromagnetism**.

Electromagnetism in Action

Scientists used Oersted's discovery to make special magnets called **electromagnets**. An electromagnet is made by coiling wire around iron or some other magnetic material. When electricity flows through the coiled wire, a strong magnetic field is produced.

When the electricity is turned off, the electromagnet turns off, too. So electromagnets are temporary. They are magnets only while electricity is flowing through them. However, they are some of the most useful magnets in the world.

A magnetic field is made when electricity (from the battery) flows through the coil wrapped around the nail. The nail becomes a magnet.

Think of all the electric cords in your home that carry electricity when plugged into electrical outlets. Cords run from lamps, the TV, and even electric guitars. Every cord has a magnetic field around it when electricity is flowing through it. When you turn on a lamp, you create a magnetic field. The cord and lamp become a magnet. The magnetism may be very weak. But it is still there.

The cord attached to this guitar has a magnetic field around it when electricity flows through it.

Chapter 3

Uses of Magnets

A Pull Toward the Future

What force could hold and move a heavy train along a track? Believe it or not, it's magnetic force.

Strong magnets can lift a whole train. Such a train is called a maglev train. "Maglev" is short for "magnetic levitation." The word "levitate" means "to lift up."

Magnets are placed on the bottom of the train. The track has a magnetic field, too. The like poles of the magnets face each other, so they repel each other. The train is lifted off the track. The train moves smoothly, quietly, and quickly.

An Electromagnetic Liftoff

In the future, magnetic levitation may become useful in a maglev rocket launch system. Powerful electromagnets will lift the rocket a few inches above a long track. Then other magnets will push and pull the rocket along the track and propel it into the atmosphere. Once the rocket reaches a speed of about 965 kilometers per hour (600 miles per hour), it will switch to regular rocket fuel.

If it works, a maglev launch system may save money for the National Aeronautics and Space Administration (NASA). The electrical power used for a maglev launch will be much cheaper than the cost of regular rocket fuel.

NASA's rocket model

wonder...

. . . how a magician can cut a rope in two, then make it one rope again?

The answer is with magnets. Two magnets are put inside the ends of two pieces of rope. Their unlike poles face each other, so the magnets attract each other. The two pieces are pulled together. They look like one rope. The magician pretends to cut this rope between the two magnets. Then the ends are placed together again. Abracadabra! The magnets attract each other once again.

Magnets Make Things Work

There are many magnets all around your house. Where are they? Some, like refrigerator magnets, are easy to see. Others, however, are much harder to spot.

Electromagnets are used in every electronic machine in your home. From telephones to CD players, electromagnets keep things running.

Did you know that the tapes used in tape players have billions of tiny magnets in them? These magnets code the sound onto the tapes. Magnets also code information onto CDs, DVDs, and floppy disks. That's why you should never place a magnet near these coded items. The force from the magnet can erase the magnetic code on the tape or disk.

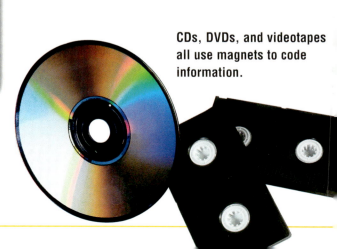

CDs, DVDs, and videotapes all use magnets to code information.

Magnets and Medicine

Sometimes doctors need to get a clear picture of what's going on inside a person's body. In some cases, magnets can help doctors get the right view without even laying a hand on a person.

An **MRI** (magnetic resonance imaging) system uses a magnetic field to produce pictures of the inside of the human body. The machine scans the person while he or she lies very still—the imaging is completely painless.

Doctors can now even scan a person's brain with an MRI device while that person is in the middle of doing an activity. These "brain mapping" images give scientists important clues about how our brains actually work.

There's no telling where the future of magnets will take us. But you can be sure it will be a push (and a pull) in the right direction!

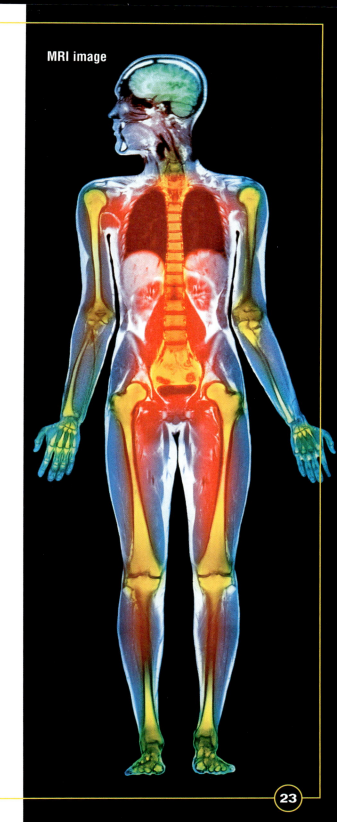

MRI image

Magnets All Around

The uses for magnets and electromagnets keep growing and growing. Many machines that run on electricity use electromagnets.

MAGNETS

A Refrigerator magnet

B Door latch

C Videotape

D Audiotape

E CD/DVD

F Board games

G Floppy disk

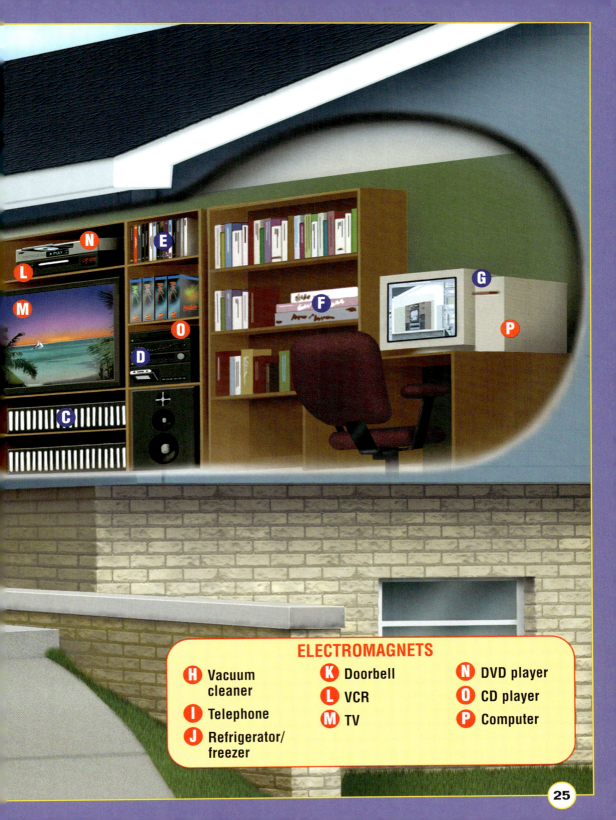

ELECTROMAGNETS

H Vacuum cleaner

I Telephone

J Refrigerator/ freezer

K Doorbell

L VCR

M TV

N DVD player

O CD player

P Computer

Inferring

You infer every day. Suppose you hear your mother calling you. You see it's six o'clock. Your stomach is growling. You might infer that it's dinnertime. Why? You put the evidence together—call, clock, hungry. In the past, those things meant it was dinnertime. You infer they mean the same thing today.

Scientists infer, too. They look at the evidence. They use their background knowledge. They really need to infer with magnetism because it's invisible. It cannot be seen or heard.

Practice the Skill

Suppose you were studying two magnets. Look at picture 1. The two magnets are the same distance from the paper clips.

Now suppose you move the paper clips closer to the magnets. Look a picture 2. Observe the evidence. Think of what you know about the strength of magnets.

Which magnet is stronger—magnet A or magnet B?

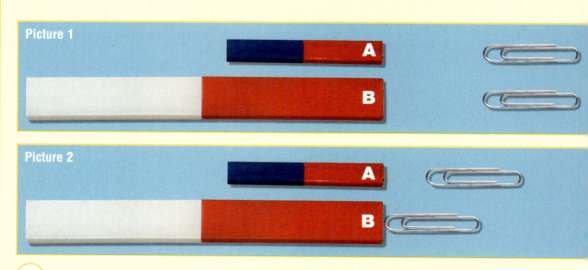

Picture 1

A

B

Picture 2

A

B

Check It Out

Suppose you place an index card between magnet A and the paper clip. The magnet still attracts the paper clip. What can you infer about the magnet's force and the index card? Set up this experiment and try it. Test different materials between the magnet and the paper clip. What can you infer about their effects on magnetism?

Make Your Own Magnets

With a few simple materials, you can make your own temporary magnet. It will lose its magnetic force very quickly. With those same materials, you can also make a permanent magnet. It will hold its force much longer.

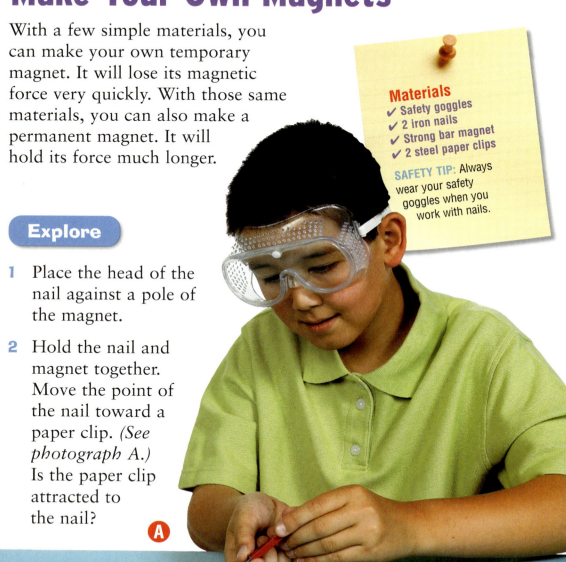

Materials
- ✓ Safety goggles
- ✓ 2 iron nails
- ✓ Strong bar magnet
- ✓ 2 steel paper clips

SAFETY TIP: Always wear your safety goggles when you work with nails.

Explore

1 Place the head of the nail against a pole of the magnet.

2 Hold the nail and magnet together. Move the point of the nail toward a paper clip. *(See photograph A.)* Is the paper clip attracted to the nail?

A

28

Hold the nail still. Slowly move the magnet away from the nail. Does the nail still attract the paper clip?

Wait a few minutes. Does the nail still attract the paper clip?

The nail was a temporary magnet.

Hold the second iron nail by the head. Stroke it with the magnet by running the magnet lengthwise from the nail's head to its point. *(See photograph B.)*

Lift the magnet and repeat this stroke. Use the same end of the magnet. Stroke in the same direction. Do this 20 times.

Place the point of the nail near the edge of the second paper clip. Is the paper clip attracted to the nail?

8 Wait a minute. Does the nail still attract the paper clip?

9 Wait 10 minutes. Does the nail still attract the paper clip?

The nail is a permanent magnet. It holds its force for a time after the stronger magnet is removed.

Think

What would happen if you stroked the nail only 5 times? What about 40 times? Do you think the strength of the magnet would be affected?

Science Notebook

MAGNETIC FORCE FACTS

- If you cut a magnet in two, you will get two magnets. Each will have a north pole and a south pole.

- A magnet can be weakened if you drop it, heat it, or hit it hard.

- You are magnetic! You have magnetism in your body. That's because there is electricity in your body. Your heart has a weak magnetic field. Your brain creates many tiny magnetic fields.

- The sun has magnetism. Sunspots on its surface have strong magnetic fields. Above these spots, fiery storms sometimes rage and burst. These storms send particles streaming toward Earth.

BOOKS TO READ

Levine, Shar, and Leslie Johnstone. *The Magnet Book*. Sterling Publishing Company, 1997.

Tocci, Salvatore. *Experiments With Magnets*. Children's Press, 2001.

Woodruff, John. *Magnetism*. Raintree Steck-Vaughn, 1998.

WEBSITES TO VISIT

The Exploratorium Science Snacks site has interesting magnetism experiments.
www.exploratorium.edu/snacks/iconmagnetism.html

You'll find more magnet facts and mini-quiz on this site.
www.school-for-champions.com/science/magnetism.htm

This "Magnet Man" site has lots fun activities, experiments, and l
my.execpc.com/~rhoadleymagindex.htm

Glossary

attract – to pull together

compass – a tool with a magnetic needle that lines up north–south

electromagnet (*i-lek-troh-MAG-net*) – a magnet made by coiling wire around iron or some other magnetic material

electromagnetism (*i-lek-troh-MAG-neh-tizm*) – the connection between electricity and magnetism

infer – to make a good guess based on evidence and background knowledge

magnet – an object with the power to attract iron and some other metals

magnetic (*mag-NET-ik*) – able to be pulled by a magnet

magnetic field (*mag-NET-ik FEELD*) – the region of force that exists around a magnet

magnetism (*MAG-neh-tizm*) – the invisible force of a magnet

migrate – to move from one place to another

MRI – letters that stand for Magnetic Resonance Imaging. MRI uses a huge magnet and radio waves to see inside the body

north pole – one of the two poles of a magnet

pole – the area of a magnet where magnetism is strongest

repel – to push away

south pole – one of the two poles of a magnet

Index